BORUT LESJAK

BREATHWORK

HEALING

STUDIO ✦ BLEST

BREATHWORK HEALING
A Beginner's Guide
#1 Grounding Tool For Your Daily Practice
By Borut Lesjak

SELF-LOVE HEALING series, book 1

www.borutlesjak.com

Copyright 2020 Borut Lesjak
Published by Studio Blest, 2020

Cover image by Witriyani Nurhasanah
Interior art by Darja Klančar
Edited by Sarah Berti

Contents

Preface

In March 2020 I had a profound vision.

I was distinctly called to create a simple, down-to-earth, and pragmatic spiritual toolbox to help us all deal with the prevalent fear characteristic of these times.

The meditative techniques and tools I'd been practicing and teaching for years were something I trusted with all my heart. I knew they could bring about a positive turn in anyone's life if only given a fair chance: a steady, dedicated focus and light-hearted work over a minimum of four weeks—one lunar cycle, indeed.

Inspired, I chose to call this healing method the *One Moon Present* formula. The formula consists of five softly powerful tools: *grounding, staying present, breathwork meditation, creative writing,* and *learning self-love.*

The central tool is *breathwork meditation,* which is based on ancient pranayama yoga and then formulated and further developed by my dear friend and teacher David Elliott and of course, by my own experience and intuition. There is no doubt in my mind that breathwork is the singular most effective tool we have at our disposal today as individuals and humanity if we honestly want to awaken to our true conscious potential and bring balance to the world.

The soft, inner core of my healing method is *self-love.* We can only ever address anything in our lives in a lasting and sustainable manner if we embrace the reality of our circumstance, whatever that may be, and offer ourselves unwavering support through our emotional upheavals and rollercoasters, confusions, denials, and resistances. I call this attitude *loving yourself through.*

In the first series of books, **Love Yourself Through**, I've collected deeply personal anecdotes related to fear, anger, and sadness. They are memoirs, assortments of intimate, transparent, and emotional stories from my real life. My choice was to open up and talk about the subtly meaningful or downright poignant events that marked, and even scarred one vulnerable boy, molding and shaping him by individual circumstance, personal responses, and in tune with untold family and societal traditions we pass on from generation to generation.

The three books of the series have a subtle, albeit specific intention: to stir, shift, and move the emotions of the reader and allow their old, deeply buried and denied memories to surface or resurface even when there was no prior awareness of any similar experiences. Sometimes we are inextricably trapped in behavioral patterns and traumatic stories that we may have inherited from our family lineage and we don't even know it because we're so used to the constant scents of negativity, abuse, or suffering in our life.

Some of the chapters overlap and touch upon either two or all three of the thematic emotions, and I wanted to include such recounts in all the books where they were applicable, even at the risk of repetition. (The three books are also available as a boxset or omnibus, titled *Love Yourself Through Fear, Anger, Sadness*.)

The reader is then heartily invited to work with the tools of the *One Moon Present* formula to open up to those past experiences and emotions in order to release energetic blocks and restore the flow of their vitality and well-being. The two tools that one needs here, *breathwork meditation* and *creative writing*, are described thoroughly in the appendix of each book. On top of that, I recorded a short 14-minute thematic breathwork meditation to be included free with each book, ready for the reader/practitioner to exchange with daily to strengthen their spiritual work.

Each of the three books of the *Love Yourself Through* series can therefore be regarded as a completely stand-alone resource to address the emotional challenges and bring about healing in life.

Nevertheless, I decided to craft another series of books, **Self-Love Healing**, that delve deeper into the theory behind the *One Moon Present* healing formula and tackle even more general questions about the definitive healing power of self-love, the essential nature of consciousness, and the ultimate fabric of our underlying reality.

Book one, *Breathwork Healing*, is a concise workbook that introduces the reader to the formula's foundational tool, *breathwork meditation*. Enough theory and practical examples are provided for anyone to safely embark on their healing journey with this book as a trusty companion. If you feel you only need a few words and a slight push to get going this book may well be the one for you to start with.

Book two, *The Healing Power of Self-Love*, is the complete manual for the committed practitioner to explore the matter further and offer the inquisitive mind elaborate clarifications about how it all really ties together. Each of the five *One Moon Present* tools is described in detail so as to leave no doubts about their inherent potential and synergetic workings. At the end of the book, a sampling of my life stories is also included, both as a demonstration of the *creative writing* tool put to practice and as inspiration for the reader to witness that it is possible to heal one's life, no matter the starting point and the weight of past burdens. The theory presented is also condensed into clear cheat sheets and a glossary of lesser-known terms is provided. This is the book for you if you feel my healing method and the energy supporting it resonate strongly with your heart and soul.

Book three, *Self-Love Healing Quick Reference*, is a compact, concentrated edition of book two, provided for the experienced practitioner of the *One Moon Present* formula who wants to keep the distilled descriptions of the five tools handy at all times to revisit, or for the pragmatic beginner who doesn't want to focus on the theory any more than necessary when embarking on their healing quest for the first time.

As a quick announcement, let me reveal that I've been working on book four, with the working title of *The Soul Syntax*. Following my deepest inner guidance and intuition, I intend to freshly revisit some of the most ancient, million-dollar questions. *Who are we? What is our purpose? What is the true nature of reality and consciousness?* To be able to address these we'll need to redefine some well-known, conventional collective viewpoints, re-program our basic wisdom and vision, and even invent or create a new cognitive syntax that is not rooted in the human mind but in the pure consciousness of the soul. Who knows, perhaps we can co-create a way out of our common vicious circle of undeserved suffering, abuse, and denial, and ascend to our true birthright and realize Heaven on Earth now.

In addition to the books, I prepared a series of breathwork meditation recordings as audiobooks, **Breathwork Healing Meditations**. They are full-length 28-minute recordings.

I can't stress enough the importance of meditating and using the breathwork recordings. In many ways, they are the primary and most elementary tools to work with as much and as often as you wish: they are both real and pragmatic. I meditate daily and I wish everyone could find the benefit, joy, and fulfillment of that in their own lives. There are no shortcuts to healing, but there is a direct route: breathwork meditation!

Whenever you feel willing to make a lasting difference in your life and the world around you, check out the meditation recordings and pick the ones that call to you. My own life changed forever the day I tried and did my first breathwork. A new hope entered then, a light arriving in the darkest hour, never to leave me again. I can feel it right now as I type this.

Are you ready?

I know you are—because you are reading this.

Introduction

Welcome to this short book about breathwork meditation and healing.

My clear intention is to help you quickly get to the essence of what healing is and how it can indeed change your life for the better. Honestly, I don't believe we need to know or understand much before we can undertake the journey to happiness, fulfilment, and well-being. We can always learn more along the way.

So how *do* we start?

By choosing to.

From the depths of the Universe, Spirit, Soul, and our Being, we make a singular choice: we *want* to heal. It doesn't matter if we don't even know what healing means at this point. We intuit it.

From then on, we will do the work. A daily practice is great, but if we can't commit to it or fail to deliver—that can be okay too, because we'll keep learning self-love and support ourselves from our heart on every step of the way, especially when it gets hard. And it will get easier. That's when we'll high-five our efforts, smile, and acknowledge how far we walked already.

What is our work of healing?

There are countless tools and it's best you choose your favorite ones to work with. Every day you can re-negotiate your allegiance. You are free. Sometimes just to sense that and experience the power of self-love is healing in itself.

Of the five *One Moon Present* tools that I've been practicing and teaching in recent years, *breathwork meditation* is ultimately the one that can stand alone. I promise you that if you only keep exchanging with it for at least seven minutes a day—or as close to that as you can get—you'll witness incredible results and openings in your life!

Without further ado: are you ready to try?

Are you choosing healing?

I intuit that you are.

Bon voyage.

Your first breathwork

At this point, I invite you to lie down on your back in a space where nobody will disturb you for ten minutes, start the meditation recording, close your eyes, and follow the guidance.

Before you do: I prepared and included a 7-minute meditation recording for you that you can freely access at this link:

omp7.breathwork.fun

Just download it to your phone or computer, or play it straight from the link.

You honestly don't need any other preparation and only ten minutes of your time.

If you're a practical person, you'll get the most out of this book right now by jumping in. But if you prefer to learn a little more before diving in, that will work too. Feel free to read on and test-drive the breathwork meditation whenever you feel comfortable doing so.

And have fun!

Breathwork meditation

I firmly believe this tool is central to healing and key to everybody's well-being in life.

When I first encountered my friend David Elliott and his healing method—of which the breathwork meditation is the centerpiece—my life was in shreds and I was ready to give up without even realizing it. Practicing this powerful, gentle, and active meditation daily—sometimes even twice in a row—restored my energy and my hope, my trust in love and in being able to *live a balanced life full of sweetness* once again—words David prescribed to me as a healing mantra.

After more than nine years of staying present and exchanging with the meditation, I can safely say that it saved my life and my soul. Yes, I know: a bold statement, but one that I can testify to and show up for.

Even if you don't feel confident about using the other four tools, breathwork meditation alone will lead you, gradually and steadily, through the hardest days into more consciousness and self-love—simply by practicing it.

How is breathwork meditation done?

Simply put, you lie down and breathe consciously through the mouth in a two-stage pattern while listening to a guiding voice and relaxing music. Near the end you start to breathe normally again, relax, and recharge. Keep your attention focused on your body and feelings, and let your emotions flow freely when they arise.

There is an abundance of detail that I could tell you here. But this tool is all about practice, so I will keep this section as short as I can. If you are weary of theory and eager to do the work, feel free to skip or skim this section—and just try the meditation. You can always return for more information when you get genuinely interested. However, I want to stress two points right from the start.

Committing to the breath

Firstly, the breathwork meditation will work only when you actually do it, and the more regularly you do it, the better. So if you are truly serious about your healing, book your time for this. It doesn't have to be long. David claims that 7 minutes a day is enough and I tend to agree.

I invite you to start working with the included 7-minute meditation recording. If harsh emotions are what you wish to address, this recording has a built-in intention for that subject. Nevertheless, my experience has been that when we surrender to the guidance of Spirit, the subjects and the objects don't matter that much. Any breathwork meditation will bring about results, when you do it.

What do I mean by that? Well, there are other recordings out there. At the time of writing this, I'm getting ready to release nine of them myself. There are over twenty of David Elliott's powerful recordings available, and I'm sure you can find a plethora of others on your own.

When you feel you are ready to go deeper with ONE MOON PRESENT formula, I recommend you start working with its full-length, 28-minute meditation, or with any of the *Love Yourself Through* meditations, which focus specifically on fear, anger, or sadness. You can find them on my website **borutlesjak.com**. (See the back of this book for more information).

> Meditate as much as you can, even when it gets gritty.

Whatever breathwork meditation you use, the important part is that you approach it diligently and respectfully. If you can't find the time or the energy to meditate every day, a few times a week is also great.

It's better not to obsess about doing it *every* day without exception. We're human beings living in a real world and anything can happen. Let's trust we'll find the time and be grateful for each occasion we're able to meditate.

Exchanging with the breath

The second point I want to make is about the quality of the practice. Like with everything else in our lives, there is not much sense in doing it just for outward appearances, just so we can tick a checkbox and be done with it. That's a waste of time and a waste of our precious hope and intent, because we dilute it with our disrespect.

Therefore, besides our dedication to the *quantity*—or the frequency of a regular and steady practice—I invite you to consider committing yourself to its *quality* as well.

> Treat breathwork as sacred.

Treat each time you practice breathwork meditation as a sacred ritual. Plan your time accordingly. Make sure nobody will disturb you. Prepare yourself a safe space where you can feel cozy and comfortable. Use essential oils if you have them and burn some sage, cedar, or palo santo wood, or perhaps light a tea candle during your practice to support your intent.

What I find of utmost importance is that we intend to consciously *exchange* with the meditation. What does that mean? It means we not only expect to receive a gift of healing from Spirit, but we are also willing to give something in return. Something worthy: our time, our attention, our presence, our awareness.

Exchange, as defined by my friend David, is not a simple quid-pro-quo though. We will not be measuring and comparing the two sides of the scales to see if we paid enough to get what we want. That's the merchant way of the mind and the love of power.

Instead, we will exchange by way of *loving*! We will cherish each and every breath we take. We will ground in our body and feelings, emotions, and thoughts. We will stay present with our whole and total experience while we meditate. We will consciously release our control in the mind and abandon ourselves to the trust in our heart.

We will melt into the moment and into a reality larger than life.

You'll see. When this is only theory with lots of big words, it doesn't do justice to the juice of experiencing it first-hand. But as soon as you will start to breathe, you'll know what I mean without a shadow of doubt.

Preparing for the meditation

The meditation is done lying down on your back, either on the floor using a yoga mat, on a massage table, or simply in your bed or on the sofa. Even outside on the grass is perfect, too.

Relax comfortably. There is no need to strain any part of your body or exert yourself in any way. The maximum effect will be achieved when you soften within and stop taking yourself and your healing process too seriously.

Why so serious? Smile.

It's best not to prop your head too much. If you do need a support for your neck, that's fine, but try to keep your air passages unobstructed so your breath and energy can flow clearly.

We'll breathe with our eyes closed. If you have a yoga eye pillow, it can assist you at calming your mind right from the start. I love the scent of lavender which is often used in those eye pillows.

Setting the intent

Just before you start with the active breathing, it's the time to set your intention, or *intent.*

Setting your intent is as easy as choosing what you want to create in your life. Here are some examples: *I want less stress. I intend my physical healing. I will write a book. I'd like to create a better relationship with my wife.*

Be specific. The more specific you get, the better. If you already know more about yourself and where you may be stuck, you can set a detailed intent. For example: *I want to address my fear of speaking in public; I want to get clear about my feelings of unworthiness and my belief that I have nothing of value to say; I intend to create more confidence and self-love around that.* That is all one single intent.

How is intending different from merely wishing something?

In the shamanic tradition revealed by Carlos Castaneda's teacher don Juan, intent is seen as an impersonal, universal force of infinite magnitude and mysterious nature which can never be understood by the mind alone. It belongs to the category of the *unknowable.*

For all practical purposes and, well, intents, we can safely say that intent is Spirit, or Universe, or Mother Nature, or even God, if you wish. In any case, we're talking about a profound feeling, a special sense, and *beckoning intent* during the meditation is a purely spiritual and abstract endeavor. Nobody understands how it is done and how it works, yet we can do it and pragmatically attest to its results in the world of everyday life.

When I lead a live meditation, right before we enter the active phase, I invite everybody to place their hands palm-down onto their chests over the heart and deeply feel within. You can do that too at this point during your meditation practice.

Ask your whole being: what is it that I want? What do I wish for more than anything else? What is my heart's and soul's true desire? What do I want to experience or express in my life? What is my mission, my life's purpose? What do I want to create and manifest, today and for the rest of my days? Also, what is it that I *don't* want? Where do I feel stuck? What do I want to change in my life? What do I want to address and heal today?

The more you circumvent the thought-controlled processes and directly feel your burning questions as long-unanswered emotions or never-addressed feelings, the more in touch you will get with intent, or Spirit—and the greater your chances of manifesting your new choices.

Let the answers come to you, effortlessly, with no obsessions. Don't chase them or cling to any old, mental-based cravings. Open up to your soul and Spirit and allow the insights and visions to flow into your attention.

Even if nothing comes up or you feel confused and don't understand the process, you can just make the answers up! No, I'm not kidding. The intent is closely tied to intuition and intuition works hand in hand with imagination—the three I's of the soul. Choose to trust the process and enjoy the ride. Make it up: what is it that you want the most in your life right now? It should be easy.

Now that you have all the questions and answers ready, combine all that you stirred up into a singular vision that you want to realize: a moment in your future when it has already happened. Your vision doesn't have to be purely visual—perhaps sounds, smells, and other perceptions came to you in a flash of intuition. Feel as if you are there, living it.

> Set your intent and feel it already manifesting.

Take spiritual note of your vision and *set the intent to manifest it*—without needing to understand how. Believe you can do that, then do it and believe you've done it. It's a matter of faith and trust in your own secret, sacred capabilities as a human being.

Proceed with the breathwork. When the time is right, the intent will ignite of itself and the manifestation will occur.

The two-stage breathing pattern

The core element of this breathwork method is the two-stage pattern of breathing. In the first phase of the meditation, which is called the active phase, you will breathe consistently through the mouth in the following manner: two inhalations, one exhalation. Open up your air passages and let the energy flow freely.

> Two breaths in. One breath out. Through the mouth.

Effectively, split the inhalation into two halves. Draw the first breath into the lower abdomen, energetically speaking, preferably all the way down to the second chakra around the sexual organs, where our emotions are often trapped. Take the second breath high into the upper chest, while lifting the energy up through the heart where it can get transmuted by our self-love. The exhalation can be natural, or only slightly accelerated, but still done through the mouth.

> Breath one: lower abdomen. Breath two: upper chest.

There will be a person breathing with you in the background of the recording, but you don't have to match their speed or intensity. You can go slower, faster, softer, or deeper. Listen to your body and energy and find your own rhythm. There is no wrong way of doing the breathwork meditation.

Nevertheless, this is not about hyperventilating, so keep it easy and steady. We want to build our energy gradually through time to create a profound and lasting effect.

> Focus on your feelings.

Some time into the breathwork, the energies will start moving and emotions will hopefully flow. That can cause us to feel colder or warmer than expected. I find it prudent to have a blanket ready just in case, even if the space is warm when you begin. Wear loose, comfortable clothing.

It's important we keep well hydrated when doing any kind of spiritual practice and breathwork is no exception. Drink clear water before you start. If you drank too much, it's okay to go to the bathroom even in the middle of meditation.

The resistance

This is a good place to mention the *resistance* that will invariably enter your practice. This method is free of rules, so everything goes: we'll be releasing our emotions, perhaps sobbing, crying, shouting, yelling, and maybe even slapping the ground with our hands in conscious outbursts.

Trust the breathwork meditation the way we perform it. Thousands upon thousands of practitioners have been doing it for decades and there is not a single recorded case of anything going south. Why would I feel the need to tell you that? Because I have witnessed many examples of people whose emotions and feelings open up so freely and wildly that they get scared of their own energy!

That is common, and you are likely to go through a whole gamut of sensations during the breathwork. Make a choice to stay with them all and keep exchanging. I promise it will lead you to a profound spiritual experience.

I see the breathwork meditation as a condensed replica of our whole life. Yes, I mean that. Everything that we keep running into during our days, we'll experience during a single breathwork session. For example, if we are prone to disliking loud rock music, we're bound to be distracted by the music that accompanies the meditation. If we hate people imposing and disrupting our inner peace, there will be someone (even if only a memory) intruding on our meditation.

In short, there will be trouble. You'll get annoyed, doubtful, scared, angry, or sad. You'll resist the breath fiercely and may reach a point when everything in you will be demanding that you cease the practice immediately.

Now, the trick is not to.

As in your life, so in breathwork—and vice versa. As you learn to enhance your consciousness, you will awaken from the resistance when you see it for what it truly is: an attempt of the mind to control the experience.

There is no greater and more direct method to train your awakening or to enhance your consciousness than the breathwork meditation, in my humble opinion. During the active phase, which lasts roughly two thirds of the total meditation time, the above mentioned resistance will test you in every which way.

> Awaken from the grip of resistance.

There is a simple common denominator to all those various kinds of resistance: the dimming of consciousness. Almost as if you were in a nightmare, you may fall prey to a single element of your own old story which will blind you to its real power—or lack thereof—and take over your whole experience.

You will fear that element, whatever it is. You may run away, fight, or resist it. And you know what they say: resistance is futile. In this case, resistance is not only futile, it is the very force that blocks your healing progress. The more you resist, the more stuck you get. As the saying goes, what you resist, persists.

Training of enlightenment

There's good news. Just as you can awaken from a nightmare and instantly free yourself from the perceived power it had over you, so too can you awaken from your resistance during breathwork. You can awaken from whatever belief you want or need to resist. This awakening is key.

It is an actual moment of enlightenment. No matter how tiny, such shards of awakened awareness work together in synergy and "their combined effect is greater than the sum of their individual effects," just as the dictionary says. Not only do we gradually gather and linearly collect all the times we awaken from our resistance, we also connect and string them together in a way that defines a brand new story, a new leaf we turn in the book of our lives.

> As in breathwork, so in daily life.

So the more resistance we encounter during our breathwork, the better our chances to enhance our consciousness. When we start looking at it that way, we may become able to welcome not only the hard times during our meditation practice, but the hard times in our daily lives. We may learn to sincerely smile at them, knowing fully well they are harbingers of change for the better. And as you probably realize, that's a huge step on our path to healing.

During a recorded breathwork session, I will support and lead you as an intuitive voice, reminding you to keep relaxing and choosing to generate ever more trust and self-love in your heart. I will repeat that your one and only task is to stay with the two-stage breathing pattern and that alone will demand of you to remain entirely present, or conscious, at all times.

If you slip and return to a normal breathing pattern, that's okay. It happens to practically everybody almost every time. No matter what happens and no matter what you feel—and how you feel about it—simply resume your two-stage rhythm commitment. That's all there is to it. No need to stop and think about it. Keep focusing your attention to the breath and your feelings.

The loving power of the breath

The beauty and magic of breathwork lies in its utter and natural simplicity. All you really need to do is to breathe and stay conscious. True, sometimes that's easier said than done, but still. Like the elegance of chess with its plain rules and complex play combinations, breathwork works miracles without you having to understand its underlying principles.

I assure you: if you learn to stay present with the breath for the whole duration of the meditation, you will learn to stay present and at the place of self-love in your daily life amidst the emotional storms and rough patches that invariably happen.

Self-love is key to healing.

The breathwork will test you and train you. It will bring up all that's been buried within you, lying dormant, blocked, forgotten yet not forgiven. The breath will open your heart and create space to generate self-love. It will invigorate and motivate you to release the flow once again. Its built-in intent will guide you internally to open up to Spirit—and when your soul and Spirit meld and work together, no other control is needed, or wanted.

The free-will choice

Only about 7 minutes of conscious breathing is needed for the mind to either relax or revolt. Which of the two happens is—in my opinion—decided by Spirit, or your soul. It is beyond anyone's control. I would support you at this point and avoid any attempts to direct the healing. We will exercise free will in its clearest form, and choose to trust the healing process unconditionally.

If the mind resists, it may be time for release. Let's follow that lead. Instead of succumbing to the resistance and fighting the triggers and effectively ourselves, let's open and warm up to the possibility of something unknown and new.

Follow Spirit's lead.

When your consciousness is ready, you'll awaken from your ordinary, nightmarish reactions caused by the resistance. You will instantly realize, on the level of feelings and awareness, that something fresh and interesting is underway. You will see your chance and choose to seize it. You will choose your healing.

Your resistance can be anything that you will deal with at that moment: from simply having to sneeze or scratch your nose, to having a hard time swallowing or taking in breaths, to wondering whether your breathing pattern and rhythm are correct, to feeling there is something bad going on and that everything in your life is falling apart, and it's your fault, and you're powerless to prevent it. The scenery of the illusion can be anything at all—but the point is simple and singular: it's just an illusion!

You are powerful beyond words, numbers, comparison, or measure. Your power is the power of love. The power of trust. The power to create anything you want to focus your attention on. The power of Spirit working through you as your soul enters your body.

The vibration of the soul

There will come a time when all of your blocks will be melted away, all of your trapped emotions released, all of your resistance used up as fuel for self-love—and all that's left will be your soul singing and dancing in your heart, body, and energy field.

This is not a black & white event, but an ongoing process. There is always something more to everything, or else life would be boring. But as soon as your mind learns to relax enough to let go of some control—and that can surely happen during your first try!—you will experience something novel in your life: a gentle tingling sensation in your hands and arms, or a soft quivering in your heart, or a pleasant electrical charge in your feet and legs. You will feel shivers running up and down your spine—and then some. Your whole body might feel as if on fire or electrified!

Witness your soul flowing into your body.

I call that the vibration of the soul. It is the interpretation we feel on the physical level when the soul enters, or starts to enter, our body. The truth is that this vibration is always there, but we can't perceive it in our ordinary mode of cognition, because the mind is too loud and grabs and completely occupies all of our finest attention. But as long as we live, and breathe, the vibration is there, within: a divine spark to animate otherwise dead matter.

It is this spark of Spirit consciousness that does the healing in our lives, if we only let it, and get out of its way. Since the vibration is ever present, our body and our whole being has the capacity of self-healing. And when we are conscious of it, it works even better—because where attention goes, energy flows. Hence the acceleration of healing that breathwork brings about as we practice it consistently.

The healing phase

The last third of the meditation is done passively, breathing naturally, through the nose or through the mouth, one breath in, one breath out. The recording will lead you to shift from the active to the passive, resting, or healing phase.

> Revert to natural breathing and recharge.

Just rest and recharge your batteries.

Your mind goes to nothing and yet you remain completely present with all of your feelings, emotions, and even thoughts that are floating around without disturbing you in the slightest. That's unconditional acceptance par excellence.

You are…

Nothing more.

Not controlling anything.

Simply observing everything.

Letting your soul—or your higher self—do the work in collaboration with Spirit.

All the generated self-love, joy, and peace—in the form of vibration—permeates your energy field and unravels the mystery of your experience, outside the limitations of space and time. Past traumas are addressed and released, even the old ones belonging to your family lineage. Future worries and fears are softened and let go from your focus, forgotten to the point of pure disinterest.

Your complete whole is concentrated in the here and now, where the power of love is.

Spontaneous emotional releases may still occur in this phase and they are always powerful. You are remaining neutral, seemingly unaffected. A spiritual momentum is building.

Here is where the long-term, lasting, sustainable healing happens.

The manifestation

At this stage, the intent you set up at the beginning of your session or extended practice will take hold, grow roots, and blossom. Bring your pure awareness to it now. Fuel it with all that you are. As soon as you sense the realness of it, it will manifest. Time-travel to that moment from your vision in the future when it has already manifested.

Feel your intent has already manifested.

You may get visions of specific steps to take in your life. Note them. You will have a chance to jot them down after the meditation—but if you urgently feel you have to write them down right now lest you forget, do it immediately. Be clear and sober enough to know whether it's just your mind trying to control you by misleading you, or whether it's the heat of your true intent spurring you into direct, creative action.

Conversely, if your visions and ideas of new steps on your path to healing frighten you or make you feel despondent and unable to fulfil your own expectations or to realize your innermost dreams—be aware that this is the mind's resistance speaking up again, trying hard to retain a foothold in a foundation you're building from scratch.

To the mind, your immense adventure of following the flow of Spirit seems absurd and downright scary. It will do its best, or worst, to keep protecting you, even from yourself. Right at this point, you will see with clarity the many deceptions and delusions of the mind. Any feelings and emotions that arise during this stage are where your next cycle of healing lies. Welcome them and don't deny them—their presence is invaluable if your desire to heal yourself is sincere.

Even through the fog of resistance, you can hope for a glance of how your visions and dreams will still come true and manifest in your life!

Return to your body

At the very end of the meditation, you'll be guided to ground and return to your body fully. You'll start doing that at your feet, by wiggling your toes. Then you'll proceed upwards over your lower legs and knees all the way to the hips. You can gently sway left-to-right here and continue upwards. Sense the internal organs and just notice how you feel in general.

Realize where you are—in your body and in your room—as you progress upwards and reach your neck and perhaps turn your head a bit. Feel into your arms and hands and now wiggle the fingers too. At last, feel your face, smile, and gently open your eyes.

And you're back. Welcome.

Ground.

Before you get up and resume your daily routine, make sure you're up for it. If the breath took you deeply into Spirit, you might feel groggy or unstable. Be careful and patient. That's also an aspect of your self-love.

If you want you can apply the grounding practice here to return to your normal self and life.

Notes of your sacred visions

Anything that may have come to you during the breathwork, write it down. Look at it as an exercise in creativity. You don't have to understand it or control it in any way. Flow with it. Later on we'll connect this to the element of *creative writing*.

Onwards ho!

After you've been exchanging with breathwork for some time in your life, your consciousness will emerge and rise in ways nobody could imagine—using the mind alone. Spirit will routinely accompany you at your daily tasks, and desirable synchronicities will follow you around. Your intuition will be powerful and trusting it will be a cinch. You will realize how natural it has become for you to base your choices—even the most crucial ones—on what your inner compass of the soul is telling you in the heart, through the language of the vibration. Yes, you will start to feel the vibration more and more often even outside of your breathing practice.

Before long, your life will be changed. A new kind of hope will well up from your soul, one that will never leave you again.

Your life starts now.

> Enjoy!

♡

Curious to learn more about all five *One Moon Present* healing tools? Order *The Healing Power of Self-Love* now and use the momentum to dive deeper!

(FREE 14-minute *One Moon Present* meditation included.)

You can get the book at this link:

hpsl.studioblest.com

Cheat Sheet: Breathwork Meditation

START

↓

#1 — Make sure nobody will disturb you

#2 — Lie down on your back and relax

#3 — Put on the meditation recording

#4 — Set the intent for the session

#5 — Do the active phase of the breathwork:

  - focus on your body and feelings
  - breathe through the mouth only
  - two breaths in and one breath out
  - breath 1 in the lower abdomen
  - breath 2 in the upper chest
  - exhale, and repeat

#6 — Switch to the passive, or healing, or resting phase:

  - breathe naturally through the nose or the mouth
  - one breath in and one breath out
  - keep resting and recharging
  - feel your desired intent being manifested

#7 — Return to your body and ground

#8 — Write down any insights or visions you had

↓

BREATHWORK MEDITATION

Author's note

Thank you for reading my book, *Breathwork Healing: A Beginner's Guide.*

In March 2020, I felt a powerful nudge as if Spirit had beckoned me, to show up and offer some direct and practical healing tools for everybody who was feeling the tremendous pressure under the harsh circumstances that had befallen us all. My first impulse was to write a book about fear and include a set of real stories from my personal life in it, alongside a description of the healing tools and the theory behind them. However, I realized that both anger and sadness should be equally recognized and touched upon, just like fear. So I set out to create a series of three books one after another. I call that series *Love Yourself Through.*

In the process of drafting the first book, I was distinctly guided to include five healing tools that work together in great synergy, and which I use daily in my own practice and teaching. Designing a cohesive, pragmatic healing formula, I chose to call it *One Moon Present.* The scope of this formula outgrew my original intention and I decided to publish it in a completely separate book, *The Healing Power of Self-Love.*

When the *The Healing Power of Self-Love* book was ready for release, I felt something was still missing: a brief, concise, quick start guide to the whole process of healing, the first stepping stone, so to speak. I did my best to produce this to-the-point booklet, *Breathwork Healing: A Beginner's Guide*, which in itself, I believe, is enough to open the avenue to anyone sincerely interested in healing.

Now you can be the judge of that in your own right and experience.

I remain humbled and grateful for your attention and for trusting my guidance. If the *breathwork meditation* practice indeed makes a difference in your life, and when you are ready for the next step on your personal healing journey, I'm confident you will find value and joy in reading the complete *The Healing Power of Self-Love* book. You can get it in your bookstore now.

All the best,
      Borut Lesjak

P.S. If you like my book and want to help a wider audience find it and work with it too, please leave an honest review!

The Healing Power of Self-Love: About the book

Does negativity rule your life? Discover a transformational approach to reclaiming joy, peace, and love.

Stuck in an endless cycle of despair? Feeling blocked at every turn? Can't seem to find the light in your day? Experienced healer, teacher, and author Borut Lesjak has spent over twenty years helping clients overcome tough situations and find their way back to hope. Now he's here to share his straight-to-the-point suite of tools to heal those deep wounds in less than one month.

The Healing Power of Self-Love: A Spiritual Guidebook: Five Grounding Tools For Your Daily Practice is a thorough and well-organized handbook to restoration using the simplest of techniques. By following Lesjak's grounded daily plan and learning to stay in the moment with this highly practical approach, you'll soon feel the fog clearing. And as your own truth becomes clearer with each day, any anger, sadness, and hurt will evaporate in favor of a potent sense of feeling in charge of your own destiny.

In *The Healing Power of Self-Love*, you'll discover:

- A full, twenty-eight-day program designed to ground you in natural practices that rekindle your happiness
- An honest, direct, and caring manual to changing your life

- Powerful daily meditation and breathwork techniques to help you feel strong
- How to reconnect with simple, earthly emotions, so you're ready to take on any challenge
- Ways to embrace life no matter how it comes, energy healing tools, and much, much more!

The Healing Power of Self-Love is a pragmatic resource packed with no-nonsense methods to assist you in recovering your wellbeing. A companion to the in-depth *Love Yourself Through* series, if you like structured roadmaps and concrete tactics all wrapped in a loving methodology, then you'll adore Borut Lesjak's straight-from-the-heart toolbox.

Buy *The Healing Power of Self-Love* and begin your transformation today!

The Healing Power of Self-Love: A sample chapter

How do you feel about your emotions?

Emotions and feelings

There are three subjects I want to address specifically while talking about emotions: the distinction between emotions and feelings, states of being, and mood. These concepts are key to the healing method I use.

Let's start by pointing out the difference between our bodily feelings and emotions. For example, fear is an emotion, but the rush of adrenaline or a clamp in the pit of your stomach is a bodily feeling that accompanies the emotion.

When we face a difficult situation—especially in our tender age—our being may employ a coping mechanism called *denial* that protects our frail ego from being overwhelmed and possibly damaged. Emotions too harsh may be swept "under the rug," or in more technical terms, into the subconsciousness, to be processed and expressed at a later, more convenient time or in a safer space.

The problems occur when we keep suppressing our emotions for too long. We could say our emotions get stuck—and *we* get stuck with them. The balance and natural course of our choices, trajectories and lives get deranged, and we're not even aware of that. From our viewpoint, everything is just fine, until the body signals us a red alert by way of pain, sickness or chronic illness.

There is a powerful connection not only between physical feelings and emotions, but also thoughts. Every heavily repeating thought, or a thought form, or a belief you entertain, will be reflected in a corresponding emotion and a body sensation or a body posture.

How do you feel about your emotions?

For example, if you routinely think of having to accomplish something to prove yourself worthy you might frequently feel the emotion of not being enough or of being empty within and you might even feel a fear of being alive. On the physical level, you may constantly slouch and feel a weight on your shoulders as if a heavy burden was actually present there, or you may feel "cold feet," or a certain emptiness or disconnection in your lower legs or ankles, almost as if your feet were not even touching the ground.

ONE MOON PRESENT formula takes all that into account and works with the interconnection of the mental, emotional, and physical levels, under the auspices of Spirit, the spiritual level.

In the example above, we may not be fully aware of our feelings of inadequacy or unworthiness, because they have perhaps been rendered subconscious. Consequently, we may live in denial of our exceeding ambition to succeed or of having to constantly compare and compete with others in order to soothe our wounded inner child and satisfy its need for recognition or praise. Many mind-created fears and problems may arise from such a condition.

The practice of ONE MOON PRESENT tools will help you become aware of where you are stuck, first on the physical level and then the emotional and mental mirror connections will become evident as well—when you are grounded and present enough and as the mind gradually releases its iron grip of control during regular breathwork meditations. Creative writing and self-love learning exercises will help you establish a new foundation for your balanced life, one full of joy and sweetness.

States of being

Some say that our emotions are located in the belly and thoughts in the head. I like to work with any coordinate system you might wish to use because we don't want to limit ourselves to the known and to what we're willing to believe. For argument's sake and for ease of explanation, let's follow the premise above.

So then, I ask you: what's in the heart?

If you say love, I agree. But what is love? Isn't love an emotion? Shouldn't it belong to the belly then?

No. You are right, because love is not an emotion. That's important. Love is a *state of being*. Just like peace and joy are. Again, we could use many coordinate systems and definitions, but deep inside, you know what I mean. There are levels of consciousness within that help us see love for what it truly is.

Not all that you feel is a feeling.

A state of being is a consequence of awareness flowing through our being. The seat of awareness is in the heart. Our soul resides in our heart for as long as we're incarnated.

Now that's also the difference between true love (or unconditional love) and a conditional love which isn't even love at all. There are energies or aspects of energies acting upon us that we mistakenly perceive as love, but we're not going to talk about that here. For our work, it is enough to say that the feeling of butterflies in the belly isn't true love—and that's why infatuations come and go, especially when we're disappointed, hurt, or heart-broken—while true love is eternal and, yes, unconditional.

Another vital consequence of the distinction between states of being, like love, and emotions, is that while emotions are strongly mirrored in physical feelings and thoughts, love isn't and can independently co-exist with any or all emotions, feelings, and thoughts. Moreover, it mixes with them, it can embrace them and even transmute them to more love—not unlike fire and any material that can burn. Healing works because love is a state of being! We'll talk more about that in the next section.

During breathwork meditation, we patiently work with our energy and trust the breath to relax our mind so we can become more clearly aware of what is what—namely, of what love's true nature is: a manifestation of our soul dancing in our body. And while we open up to our stuck emotions and deal with our old hurts and physical discomforts, we still stay fully present with our love at all times. As we do that, we become aware of love and perceive it as a vibration which begins in the heart and then spreads throughout the body. We let it embrace all of our ailments, our imperfections and our problems, to make them go away—and love can really do that!

I firmly believe it is crucial for our self-healing method to work in a lasting and sustainable manner, that we do all our work ourselves, internally, by inviting the external agent—Spirit, Universe, God, Soul—to enter our sacred temple, the body. The responsibility and the power rest with us. It's all in our hands, and yet it isn't. It's a paradox that the mind is unable to unravel, and luckily, it never has to. It is enough to simply stay with the breath and remain conscious of everything we experience. Something larger than us—which is at the same time part of us—takes over and makes healing happen.

Mood

When I say mood, I'm not talking only about mood swings or moodiness. Simply put, mood is how we feel about our day, and also how we feel about our feelings, emotions, thoughts, ourselves, our lives and the world in general. It's a complex conglomerate of subtle, all-inclusive, omni-directional perception, both externally and internally oriented. It's where our feelings, emotions, and thoughts come together with our awareness.

For our healing process, it's vital we warm up to the idea that our mood is something that we may be able to choose, or intend—at least on some levels. It's not just an arbitrary emotional state that we get thrown into by circumstances. Mood is our response to the circumstances, and it is where our character shows—and depending on the clarity of our consciousness, we can avoid many pitfalls of prejudice, convictions, beliefs, and other programming, when we choose our responses to life's situations.

Another way of talking about mood is to liken it to weather. Of course, mood swings have been compared to weather before, nothing new here. The point I'm illustrating with this example is how the element of choice comes into the game—something we'll go deeper into in the next section. The feelings, emotions, and thoughts themselves may be more or less outside of our control, like most circumstances generally are. And our mood on a certain level may still not be something we can create or direct at will. But our perception of, and our response to our mood is already one level closer to the place of our command or choice.

> You are layered like a dream within a dream.

Back to weather. When it rains, we can't stop that. What we can do is make a choice: either we try to stay dry or we could choose to dance and sing in the rain. But even if we choose the former, we might still get wet involuntarily—it was obviously outside of our control. *Now* what we *can* choose is our response to what happened to us: we can get upset or just unhappy, or we can choose not to linger on it for long and instead change our clothes and get on with our day.

Going deeper, perhaps rainy weather makes us sad and such a response is beyond our choice—because of our subconscious programming. Or we may be trying hard to like the cold weather, but keep failing at it. And then we get disappointed by our failure to stay positive in that regard. So many levels there!

If we look at our feelings, emotions, and thoughts instead of the weather phenomena now, we may observe we have a similar response to them: our mood is our response. And then we have a response to our mood, which is mood again, but on another level. For example, if we get angry with our child for getting wet in the rain we may feel guilty because of our perhaps unwarranted or exaggerated anger. We may feel inadequate as a parent or even a failure as a human being, if we are inclined or programmed that way. In turn, our mood would probably shift to heavy and unpleasant. And if that is something that we experience often, we may have already anticipated it happening and feared it, or we may feel a leaden weight of being stuck in a vicious circle with seemingly no way out.

Thus, we've come a long way from an innocent accident of getting wet in the rain, through many levels of responses to a response (i.e. many levels of moods), and ultimately to a somber mood of "everything is wrong in the world" in a matter of seconds. The more we struggle to stay afloat, the more we sink into the quicksand of—trickery of the programming!

Before we discuss a way out of this nightmare, in the next section, one last definition. *Prevalent mood* is the general feeling about our life that we've settled upon: the way we see ourselves and our role in the world. For the example above, the prevalent mood could be depression. And the way we create and reinforce our prevalent mood to ourselves by the internal dialog we incessantly repeat in the mind, is what I call "our old story."

So how do we get out of there? The way out is through.

Summary

What did we learn in this section?

Feelings and emotions are not the same thing, even though they mirror each other, and they mirror thoughts as well. Love isn't an emotion but a state of being. It comes with awareness and coexists with emotions and uplifts them. Mood is our current, inner response to all of the above. There are countless levels of mood as we keep responding to our own responses. Prevalent mood is our overall response to ourselves and life in general. In the next section, we'll consider whether we are free to choose our prevalent mood unconditionally.

♡

Get *The Healing Power of Self-Love* in your favorite bookstore now at **hpsl.studioblest.com** and continue reading about the grand mystery of awareness and healing!

Find out more about the ONE MOON PRESENT formula and my healing practice, other books, meditations, tools, and stay connected on **borutlesjak.com**.

Glossary

These definitions are merely guidelines or inspiration to help you open up to a new-story point of view. Some are included to clarify the more obscure or less common terms (e.g. *wounded inner child, pranayama, claircognizance*) and some are listed to expand the standard definitions of well-known terms, which are used in the *One Moon Present* book and formula in a new or different way (e.g. *mind, awareness, mood*).

abuse — Any expression or experience stemming from diminished *consciousness* and lack of *self-love* resulting in unbalanced *exchange*.

awakening — A temporary expansion of your *awareness*. Exercising awakening by daily *meditation* will grow your potential for a heightened *consciousness*.

awareness — Your essence and the essence of all there is: the stuff your soul is made of. Also, your knowing of the world around you and your attention to it.

belief — A mind-based *thought* form that focuses your energy to uphold your *old story*.

block — An interruption of the flow of your life energy, usually a consequence of a past trauma or inherited pattern of behavior. *Consciousness* softens and releases blocks.

breathwork — A central tool of the ONE MOON PRESENT formula. Daily practice of breathwork will help you nurture your *awareness* and *self-love*. The breath, when you *exchange* with it, carries the gentle yet unstoppable power of softening your emotional *blocks* and restoring your energy *flow*.

chi (or life force) — The energy flowing through your being for as long as you're alive. It can get obstructed or blocked. *Healing* restores its flow.

clairaudience — Intuitive hearing and speaking, based in the throat chakra, connected to the thyroid gland.

claircognizance — Intuitive knowing, based in the crown chakra, connected to the pineal gland.

clairsentience — Intuitive feeling, based in the heart chakra, connected to the thymus gland.

clairvoyance — Intuitive seeing, based in the third-eye chakra, connected to the eyes and the pituitary gland.

clarity — The opposite of *confusion*.

confusion — A mind-based perceived lack of sense, direction, and capacity for free-will choice. *Consciousness* clears confusion.

consciousness — A sublime, divine awareness of being aware, a state of being *awakened* or *enlightened*, a non-linear *presence* with all there is, externally and internally.

control (or the mind's control) — A tendency of the *mind* to protect your being by trying to direct absolutely everything.

creativity — A direct route to *healing* by transcending your *beliefs* and using *intuition* as the compass of your *soul* to guide your *free-will* choices and create your *new-story reality*.

denial — A natural mechanism for coping with an unbearable experience. May impede the process of *healing* when exaggerated. *Consciousness* exposes denial.

ego — An identification with anything less than the whole of who you are. Tightly coupled with the *mind*, the ego personality works tirelessly to protect itself—and you—against countless potentially harmful *beliefs*. May convince you to obsessively focus on fear, anger, or sadness and thus expend most of your daily energy for upholding your *old story* instead of creating healing in your life.

emotion — A movement of energy in your nervous system and your field of energy. Emotions can get stuck and may *block* your *flow* of *chi*, resulting in chronic fatigue, stress, discomfort or illness.

energy — The underlying source of all material existence, as opposed to *awareness*, the underlying source of energy, but also of non-physical existence.

enlightenment — Clarity and *presence* of awakened *consciousness*. The practice of ONE MOON PRESENT tools gives rise to frequent, tiny, quantum enlightenments.

exchange — Your *awareness* of the interconnecting *flow* of all there is. A sacred willingness to expand and open up to life, even in the midst of *resistance*. Giving and receiving freely of the essence of yourself, others, and the Universe. An unbalanced exchange *blocks* the *flow*.

feeling — A physical, bodily sensation, as opposed to an *emotion* based in your energy field and the nervous system. Feelings, emotions, and also thoughts are tightly coupled.

flow (or energy flow) — A natural state of all existence. When your flow is obstructed or *blocked* by stuck *emotions*, past traumas, or inherited *programs*, you experience a rift in *consciousness* where your *wounded inner child* gets disconnected from the whole, and you may need *healing*.

free will — Your soul-based capacity for making *choices* and creating *reality*. Can be obscured and confused by programming, patterns of behavior, and denial. *Consciousness* reveals and illuminates free will.

God — A common name for an unknowable source of all there is. *Spirit, Universe*.

gratitude — A direct route to *healing* by opening your heart, learning *self-love*, and balancing your *exchange* through appreciation.

grounding — A sacred ritual of pausing and connecting to *Mother Earth* and soul-based *reality*.

healing — A process of improving the quality of your life by learning who you are and how to love yourself.

humor — A direct route to *healing* by opening up to the *flow* and letting go of *control*.

inspiration — An avenue of soul-based communication that can be freely used against all odds, even through your worst mind-based *confusion*, *denial*, and *resistance*. *Breathwork* is an avenue to inspiration.

intent — An unknowable force of manifesting reality which you can't control but you can still use it in a mysterious way, especially during meditation.

intuition — A soul-based language of conscious *creativity*, as opposed to mind-based *thoughts*. A limitless, irreducible, and infallible expression of your *free will*. Your *soul* may intuitively communicate to and through you in many ways; also see *clairaudience, clairvoyance, clairsentience, claircognizance*.

love — A *state of being*, neither a *feeling/emotion* in the belly nor a *thought* in the head. Can co-exist with any feelings, emotions, and thoughts at the same time.

manifesting — Creating your reality by focusing your energy. It can be a *free-will* choice of opening up to and bringing in more *healing, love*, and universal *exchange* of Oneness, or a mind-based choice, upholding the diminished reality of your *old story*.

meditation — Any consistent and dedicated practice of *grounding* and relaxing the mind, and opening up to faith and your *soul* entering your body.

mind — A complex energetic organ of perception with the capacity of creating a virtual, mind-based reality, as opposed to a true, soul-based one. Neither negative nor positive, it can and usually is usurped and programmed by the stuck energies of past traumas to keep creating a mind-based *old story* of *suffering*.

mood — A current, inner response to your *feelings*, *emotions*, *thoughts*, and *state of being*. Also, a response to other responses in a layered fashion.

Mother Earth — A matrix for Humanity. A living, sentient being, unconditionally loving and supporting all living on Her.

negative — Anything we define by resisting it, fighting it, or running away from it.

new story — A story you create by choice to bring about a change in life.

old story — A story you repeat to yourself and which may keep you stuck in life.

pranayama — An ancient, yogic *meditation* technique based on conscious breathing, with countless variants.

presence — A conscious *clarity* about what is what, on the level of *awareness*, not thoughts.

prevalent mood — An overall response to yourself and life in general. A core building block of your *old (or new) story*.

quantum breath — A simple breathing exercise to train your *presence*. See the section on *staying present*.

reality — A relative and subjective manifestation that you maintain by focusing your attention. An interpretation of your internal and external perception. Either a mind-based construct, upholding your old story, or a soul-based conscious exchange with Spirit, opening your life to your purpose and fulfilment of your mission. Or an interplay of the two.

resistance — Any *feeling*, *emotion*, *thought*, or *mood* of *negativity*— or *positivity*—that may attempt to disrupt your process of *healing* by convincing you otherwise. *Consciousness* dispels resistance.

self-love — An unconditional embrace of your *wounded inner child*. A *state of being* when you love a troubling part of yourself and feel loved unconditionally.

soul — An inextricable aspect of *Spirit* pertaining to an individual being or many (potentially simultaneous) incarnations of a Being.

Spirit — An all-encompassing, eternal *awareness* and *consciousness* of all there is. *God*, *Universe*.

spiritual — An aspect of absolutely everything in life that is touched by the *reality* of *consciousness*.

state of being — A consequence of *awareness* flowing through our being, e.g. love, joy, peace. Sometimes confused with *feelings*, *emotions*, or *thoughts*.

suffering — A mind-based choice to diminish your experience against the free will of your soul.

thought — A unit of mind-based *energy* which can be focused in tune with your *free-will* choices or against them, thus accelerating or impeding your *healing* process.

vibration — A physical and energetic sensation of your *soul* or *Spirit* moving through your body and your being.

vicious circle — See *vicious circle*. *Healing* transmutes a vicious circle into a virtuous spiral.

wounded inner child — A part of you that is disconnected from your whole being as a consequence of a past trauma or a rough experience you couldn't cope with. When your wounded inner child gets triggered, your *consciousness* will shrink and your choices will be limited by *confusion*, *resistance*, and *denial*.

FREE Borut Lesjak starter healing kit

Subscribe to our newsletter at **borutlesjak.com** to keep in touch and be advised of the forthcoming sequels and other healing materials—get your **FREE Borut Lesjak's healing quick start kit**, including the **complete** *Breathwork Healing* **e-book**, the **7-minute** *One Moon Present* **breathwork meditation**, and the *One Moon Present* **formula's beautifully designed set of cheat sheets**. You will also receive invitations to **beta-reader copies** of my new books, and an occasional, never-before published chapter from both behind the scenes and from the great beyond.

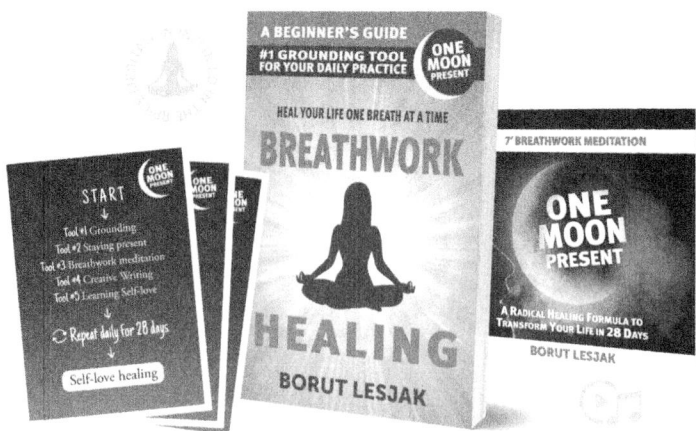

If *The Healing Power of Self-Love* moved you a step forward on your path of healing, please take a moment to quickly rate the book or even write a brief review—ratings and reviews *truly* help grateful authors reach wider audiences and form growing communities of mutual trust—in love.

DO YOU WISH TO MEDITATE MORE?

Are you ready *and* willing to boost your daily spiritual practice?

The full-length, 28-minute meditation, *One Moon Present Breathwork Meditation* has been crafted under the auspices of Spirit and imbued with a clear intent of helping you honestly detect, lovingly address, and gently release any negativity in your life.

You can get the meditation at this link:

omp.breathwork.fun

Love Yourself Through series

If you seek healing in your life and are looking for a practical account from the trenches of somebody else's expansion that may inspire you to take your next steps, *Love Yourself Through* is one such report. Its formula continues where *One Moon Present* left off. Check out the series on **borutlesjak.com**, where an ever-growing compilation of transparent, personal stories are shared, working in conjunction with the five practical tools of ONE MOON PRESENT.

Love Yourself Through is a series of direct, hands-on workbooks with clearly defined tools, daily tasks, and goals. An ancient breathwork technique as well as other earth-grounded modalities are the integral ingredients to a conclusive formula called ONE MOON PRESENT that will transform your life within a single moon cycle. With a potent collection of inspirational stories as the main core of the *Love Yourself Through* books, and a practical, step-by-step guide, you will feel inspired and confident to address and recast blocked feelings or suppressed emotions, whether fear, anger or sadness. Revolutionize your life and experience well-being, health, joy, peace, and love every day—as a rule—not as an exception.

"Borut Lesjak is amazing and so are his gifts! He speaks his truth with pure love and first-hand experience, bringing to us the compassion and mission of a true healer striving to benefit humanity. He gets to the point and shares what works!"
—*Randi Maggid, vibrational shaman, breathwork healer & author*

You can get the three-book box set at this link:

lyt.studioblest.com

About the author

Borut Lesjak is an intuitive healer and author from Slovenia. Since childhood, he has been drawn to grok the mystery of existence. During the vulnerable years of his carefree youth, he awakened to the awareness of death and life, discovering a gift of claircognizance. Life hard-rocked the sensitive adult Lesjak to a state of hopeless haze until he ignited an inner choice to heal himself. Breathwork meditation coupled with creative expression opened his heart and mind to restore his innocence. Grounded by realness larger than life, he found his calling by bringing clarity, compassion, integration, and joy to this beloved planet for all to experience.

After residing and working in Australia, USA, Mexico, and Paris, France, he is now back in Slovenia growing roots with his wife and three children, offering healing work and writing books. He loves to dream, drive, travel, and hike. He is having fun.

You can connect with Borut at **borutlesjak.com** or stalk him on social media. He self-publishes, and personally reads and responds to his email at **borut@borutlesjak.com**.

"Borut Lesjak is a force of nature, and his unflinching, radical commitment to healing, growth and the transformative power of love is brought to life in *The Snowflake*, a gentle tale about the journey towards union and the magic of harmony with the wild world."

—*Sarah Berti, mythmaker, author of the Helix Library Mythos*

Printed in Great Britain
by Amazon

45822655R00036